PARAMAHANSA YOGANANDA
(1893–1952)

How-to-Live Series

LIVING FEARLESSLY

BRINGING OUT YOUR INNER SOUL STRENGTH

Selections from the talks and writings of
Paramahansa Yogananda

Self-Realization Fellowship
FOUNDED 1920
Paramahansa Yogananda

ABOUT THIS BOOK: *Living Fearlessly: Bringing Out Your Inner Soul Strength* is a compilation of selections from Paramahansa Yogananda's writings, lectures, and informal talks. These originally appeared in his books, in articles in *Self-Realization* (the magazine he founded in 1925), in the three anthologies of his collected talks and essays, and in other Self-Realization Fellowship publications.

Authorized by the International Publications Council of
SELF-REALIZATION FELLOWSHIP
3880 San Rafael Avenue
Los Angeles, California 90065-3298

The Self-Realization Fellowship name and emblem (shown above) appear on all SRF books, recordings, and other publications, assuring the reader that a work originates with the society established by Paramahansa Yogananda and faithfully conveys his teachings.

Library of Congress Cataloging-in-Publication Data

Yogananda, Paramahansa, 1893-1952.
  Living fearlessly : bringing out your inner soul strength : selections from the talks and writings of Paramahansa Yogananda. — 1st ed.
    p. cm. — (How-to-live series)
  ISBN-13: 978-0-87612-469-7
  ISBN-10: 0-87612-469-4
 I. Spiritual life. I. Title. II. Series.
BP605.S43 Y62 2003
294.5'44 — dc21

                    2003012236

Printed in the United States of America
1718-J771

*I*n his *Autobiography of a Yogi,* Paramahansa Yogananda related the following conversation with his guru, Swami Sri Yukteswar:

"*Guruji, I would like to hear some stories of your childhood.*"

"*I will tell you a few — each one with a moral!*" Sri Yukteswar's eyes twinkled with his warning.

"*My mother once tried to frighten me with an appalling story of a ghost in a dark chamber. I went there immediately, and expressed my disappointment at having missed the ghost. Mother never told me another horror tale.*

"*Moral: Look fear in the face and it will cease to trouble you.*"

CONTENTS

PREFACE

"Self-realization is the knowing—in body, mind, and soul—that we are one with the omnipresence of God; that we do not have to pray that it come to us, that we are not merely near it at all times, but that God's omnipresence is our omnipresence; that we are just as much a part of Him now as we ever will be. All we have to do is improve our knowing."

—Paramahansa Yogananda

In his "how-to-live" teachings, Paramahansa Yogananda has given to people of all cultures, races, and creeds the means to free themselves from physical, mental, and spiritual inharmonies—to create for themselves a life of enduring happiness and all-round success.

The books in this series present Paramahansaji's how-to-live wisdom on many subjects—in his own words and in those of his close disciples—providing readers with spiritual insight and practical keys for bringing into daily life the inner balance and harmony that is the essence of yoga. Through the practice of meditation and the universal principles of right action and right attitude highlighted in these books, one can experience every moment as an opportunity to grow in awareness of the Divine.

While each book addresses a distinct topic, one message resonates throughout the series: *Seek God first*. Whether speaking of creating fulfilling relationships, raising spiritual children, overcoming self-defeating habits, or any of the other myriad goals and challenges of modern living, Paramahansa Yogananda again and again refocuses our attention towards life's highest attainment: Self-realization—knowing our true nature as divine beings. Through the inspiration and encouragement of his teachings, we learn how to live a truly victorious life—transcending limitations, fear, and suffering—by awakening to the infinite power and joy of our real Self: the soul.

—*Self-Realization Fellowship*

LIVING
FEARLESSLY

Make Your Life a Divine Adventure

Life is the greatest adventure imaginable. Although some lives are without much interest and excitement, others are full of extraordinary experiences....Yet to fathom the nature of Spirit is the greatest adventure in this universe....

Befriend Yourself by Asserting Your Divine Nature

An adventure with wild animals in South Africa is nothing compared to the adventure of life itself. No other tale in history is as inter-

---

Extracts from "Man's Greatest Adventure," a talk given at Self-Realization Fellowship International Headquarters, Los Angeles. The complete talk appears in *Man's Eternal Quest* (Paramahansa Yogananda's *Collected Talks and Essays, Volume I*).

esting. Man with his intelligence knows how to protect himself against animals, but he doesn't know how to protect himself against his own bad habits and evil ways. The greatest of all enemies of man is himself. More than personal or national enemies, more than germs, bombs, or any other threat, man should fear himself when he is wrong. To remain in ignorance of your divine nature and to be overpowered by bad habits is to make an enemy of your own self. The best way to be successful in this adventure of life is to be your own friend. Krishna said: "The Self is the friend of the (transformed) self, but the enemy of the unregenerate self."*

The Subtle Enemies

It is easy to picture ourselves starting off to explore some wild and unknown country. If we are going by ship we want a lifeboat with us;

---

*Bhagavad Gita VI:6

should the steamer sink, we know we can get into the boat and save ourselves. But in so many of life's experiences there seems to be a leak in our lifeboat, no matter what precautions we have taken.

In a jungle infested with animals you can take reasonable care against them, but subtle dangers are more difficult to overcome. How to protect oneself against a barrage of germs? Millions are floating around us all the time....Nature forms a restraining wall of cells around them, but it is effective only so long as the body can keep up its resistance. This struggle of life goes on constantly in the unseen jungle of life within!...

In order to go safely through this jungle of life you must equip yourself with the proper weapons....The wise man who is armed against all forms of warfare—against disease, against destiny and karma, against all evil thoughts and habits—becomes the victor in this adventure. It requires carefulness and, in addition, the adoption of certain methods by which we can overcome our enemies....

God has given us one tremendous instrument of protection—more powerful than machine guns, electricity, poison gas, or any medicine—the mind. It is the mind that must be strengthened....An important part of the adventure of life is to get hold of the mind, and to keep that controlled mind constantly attuned to the Lord. This is the secret of a happy, successful existence....It comes by exercising mind power and by attuning the mind to God through meditation....The easiest way to overcome disease, disappointments, and disasters is to be in constant attunement with God.

Supreme Help Comes From Tuning in With Spirit

We are babes in the woods of life, forced to learn by our own experiences and troubles, stumbling into pitfalls of sickness and wrong habits. Again and again we have to raise our voices for help. But the Supreme Help comes from tuning in with Spirit.

Whenever you are in trouble, pray: "Lord, You are within me and all around me. I am in the castle of Thy presence. I have been struggling through life, surrounded by many kinds of deadly enemies. I now see that they are not really agents for my destruction; You have put me on earth to test my power. I am going through these tests only to prove myself. I am game to fight the evils that surround me; I will vanquish them by the almightiness of Your presence. And when I shall have passed through the adventure of this life I will say: 'Lord, it was hard to be brave and fight; but the greater my terror, the greater was the strength within me, given by You, by which I conquered and realized that I am made in Your image. You are the King of this universe and I am Your child, a prince of the universe. What have I to fear?'"

As soon as you realize you have been born a human being you have everything to fear. There seems to be no escape. No matter what precautions you take, there is always a misstep somewhere. Your only security is in God. Whether you are in the African jungle or at war or racked by disease and poverty, just say to the Lord, and believe: "I am in the armored car of Your presence, moving across the battlefield of life. I am protected."

There is no other way to be safe. Use common sense and trust fully in God. I am not suggesting something eccentric; I am urging you to affirm and believe, no matter what happens, in this truth: "Lord, it is You alone who can help me." So many have fallen into ruts of disease and wrong habits and have not pulled themselves out. Never say you cannot escape. Your misfortune is only for a time. The failure of one life is not the measure of whether or not you are a success. The attitude of the conquering man is unafraid: "I am a child of God. I have nothing to fear." So fear nothing. Life and death are only different processes of your consciousness.

Bring Out the Buried Soul Immortality Within You

Everything the Lord has created is to try us, to bring out the buried soul immortality within us. That is the adventure of life, the one purpose of life. And everyone's adventure is different, unique. You should be prepared to deal with all problems of health, mind, and soul by common-sense methods and faith in God, knowing that in life or death your soul remains unconquered. You can never die. "No weapon can pierce the soul; no fire can burn it; no water can moisten it; nor can any wind wither it.... The soul is immutable, all-permeating, ever calm, and immovable."* You are eternally the image of Spirit.

* Bhagavad Gita II:23–24.

Is it not freeing to the mind to know that death cannot kill us? When disease comes and the body stops working, the soul thinks, "I am dead!" But the Lord shakes the soul and says: "What is the matter with you? You are not dead. Are you not still thinking?" A soldier is walking along and a bomb shatters his body. His soul cries, "Oh, I am killed, Lord!" And God says, "Of course not! Are you not talking to Me? Nothing can destroy you, My child. You are dreaming." Then the soul realizes: "This is not so terrible. It was only my temporary earth-life consciousness of being a physical body that made losing it seem the end of me. I had forgotten that I am the eternal soul."

The Goal of Our Life-Adventure

True yogis are able to control the mind under all circumstances. When that perfection is reached, you are free. Then you know life is a divine adventure. Jesus and other great souls have proved this....

You will finish this life-adventure only when you conquer its dangers by your will power and mind power, as did the Great Ones. Then you will look back and say: "Lord, it was a pretty bad experience. I came near failing, but now I am in the safety of Your presence forever."

We can see life as a wonderful adventure when the Lord finally says, "All those terrifying experiences are over. I am with you evermore. Nothing can harm you."

Man is playing at life like a child, but his mind grows stronger through fighting sickness and troubles. Anything that weakens your mind is your greatest enemy, and whatever strengthens your mind is your haven. Laugh at any trouble that comes....Know you are everlasting in the Lord.

THOUGHTS FOR THE FEARLESS SOUL

Meet everybody and every circumstance on the battlefield of life with the courage of a hero and the smile of a conqueror.

---•◆•---

You are a child of God. What have you to fear?

---•◆•---

We must have faith in our ability, and hope in the triumph of a righteous cause. If we do not possess these qualities, we must create them in our own minds through concentration. This can be accomplished by determined and long-continued practice.

Fortunately, we can start practicing any time and any place, concentrating upon developing those good qualities in which we are defective. If we are lacking in will power, let us concentrate upon that, and through conscious effort we shall be able to create strong will power in ourselves. If we want to relieve ourselves of fear, we should meditate upon courage, and in due time we shall be freed from the bondage of fear.

Through concentration and meditation we make ourselves powerful.

——— • ———

There is always a way out of your trouble; and if you take the time to think clearly, to think how to get rid of the cause of your anxiety instead of just worrying about it, you become a master.

——— • ———

Always affirm: "Nothing can hurt me. Nothing can ruffle me." Realize that you are as good

13

as the best man, as powerful as the strongest man. You must have more faith in yourself.

———•◆•———

One who has faith in the divinity of his own soul, his true nature, and who has love for God and faith in His omnipotence finds quick freedom from suffering.... The light of faith ushers his consciousness from the dark realm of mortal limitation into the kingdom of immortality.

———•◆•———

Faith means knowledge and conviction that we are made in the image of God. When we are attuned to His consciousness within us, we can create worlds. Remember, in your will lies the almighty power of God.

Practical Antidotes for Fear and Worry

Many people come to me to talk about their worries. I urge them to sit quietly, meditate, and pray; and after feeling calmness within, to think of the alternate ways by which the problem can be solved or eliminated. When the mind is calm in God, when the faith is strong in God, they find a solution to their problem. Merely ignoring problems won't solve them, but neither will worrying about them.

Meditate until you become calm; then put your mind on your problem and pray deeply for God's help. Concentrate on the problem and you will find a solution without going through the terrible strain of worry....

Remember, greater than a million reasonings of the mind is to sit and meditate upon God until you feel calmness within. Then say to the Lord, "I can't solve my problem alone, even if I thought a zillion different thoughts; but I can solve it by placing it in Your hands, asking first for Your guidance, and then following through by thinking out the various angles for a possible solution."

God does help those who help themselves. When your mind is calm and filled with faith after praying to God in meditation, you are able to see various answers to your problems; and because your mind is calm, you are capable of picking out the best solution. Follow that solution, and you will meet with success. This is applying the science of religion in your daily life.

———— • ————

Fear develops a malignant magnetism by which it draws to itself the objects feared, just as a magnet draws a piece of iron, and thus increases our miseries. Fear intensifies and magnifies our physical pain and mental agonies a hundredfold, and is destructive to the heart, nervous system, and brain. It paralyzes mental initiative, courage, judgment, common sense, will power, and the sense-to-avert-danger consciousness. Fear contaminates strong imagination and feeling, and through them may so influence the subconscious mind as to completely vanquish the willing efforts of the conscious mind. Fear throws a veil on intuition, shrouding the almighty power of your natural confidence that springs intuitively from the all-conquering soul....

When you are threatened with the possibility of injury, do not throttle your all-producing inner machine of consciousness with mental fear. Rather, use your fear as a stimulus to manipulate your inner machine of consciousness to produce some mental device that will instantaneously remove the cause of fear. These mental devices to escape fear are so numerous that they have to be specially manufactured in the all-accomplishing machine of consciousness according to the specific and extraordinary needs of an individual. So when you are threatened by danger or any hurtful experience, do not sit idly. Do something calmly, do something quickly, *but do something*, mustering all the power of your will and judgment. Will power is the steam or motive power that works the machine of activity.

Uproot Fear From Within by Concentration on Courage

Fear of failure or sickness is cultivated by turning over such thoughts in the conscious mind until they become rooted in the subconscious and finally in the superconscious. Then the superconsciously and subconsciously rooted fear begins to germinate and fill the conscious mind with fear plants that are not so easy to destroy as the original thought would have been, and these eventually bear their poisonous, death-dealing fruits.

If you are unable to dislodge by conscious will a haunting fear of ill health or of failure, keep on diverting your attention by reading interesting books that absorb your attention; or even indulge in harmless amusements. Then the mind will forget to haunt itself with fear. Next make your mind take up the shovels of different mental devices and dig out from the soil of your daily life the root causes of failure and ill health.

Uproot them from within by forceful concentration upon courage, and by shifting your consciousness to the absolute peace of God within. When you are able psychologically to uproot the negative quality of fear, then divert your attention to getting busy with positive methods of acquiring prosperity and health.

REMOVING THE STATIC OF
FEAR FROM THE MIND

Often when you are trying to tune in a radio station, static comes in and disturbs the program you are trying to hear. Likewise, when you are trying to accomplish some personal transformation in your heart, "static" may interrupt your progress. That static is your bad habits.

Fear is another form of static that affects your mind radio. Like good and bad habits, fear can be both constructive and destructive. For example, when a wife says, "My husband will be displeased if I go out this evening; therefore I won't go," she

---

Extracts from "Eliminating the Static of Fear From the Mind Radio," a talk given at Self-Realization Fellowship Temple, Encinitas, California. The complete talk appears in *Man's Eternal Quest* (Paramahansa Yogananda's *Collected Talks and Essays, Volume I*).

is motivated by loving fear, which is constructive. Loving fear and slavish fear are different. I am speaking of loving fear, which makes one cautious lest he hurt someone unnecessarily. Slavish fear paralyzes the will. Family members should entertain only loving fear, and never be afraid to speak truth to one another. To perform dutiful actions or sacrifice your own wishes out of love for another person is much better than to do so out of fear. And when you refrain from breaking divine laws, it should be out of love for God, not from fear of punishment.

Fear Cannot Enter a Quiet Heart

Fear comes from the heart. If ever you feel overcome by dread of some illness or accident, you should inhale and exhale deeply, slowly, and rhythmically several times, relaxing with each exhalation. This helps the circulation to become normal. If your heart is truly quiet you cannot feel fear at all.

Anxieties are awakened in the heart through the consciousness of pain; hence fear is dependent on some prior experience — perhaps you once fell and broke your leg, and so you learned to dread a repetition of that experience. When you dwell on such an apprehension your will is paralyzed, and your nerves also, and you may indeed fall again and break your leg. Furthermore, when your heart becomes paralyzed by fear, your vitality is low and disease germs get a chance to invade your body.

Be Cautious But Not Fearful

There is hardly anyone who does not fear disease. Fear was given to man as a cautionary device to spare him pain; it is not meant to be cultivated and abused. Overindulgence in fear only cripples our efforts to ward off difficulties.

Cautious fear is wise, as when, knowing the principles of right diet, you reason, "I won't eat that cake, because it is not good for me." But unreasoning apprehension is a cause of disease; it is the real germ of all sickness. Dread of disease precipitates disease. Through the very thought of sickness you bring it on yourself. If you are constantly afraid of catching a cold, you will be more susceptible to it, no matter what you do to prevent it.

Do not paralyze your will and nerves with fear. When anxiety persists in spite of your will, you are helping to create the very experience you are dreading.

Also, it is unwise to associate more than is necessary and considerate with people who constantly discuss their own and others' ailments and infirmities; this dwelling on the subject may sow seeds of apprehension in your mind. Those who are worried they are going to succumb to tuberculosis, cancer, heart trouble, should cast out this fear, lest it bring about the unwelcome condition.

Those who are already sick and infirm need as pleasant an environment as possible, among people who have a strong and positive nature, to encourage them in positive thoughts and feelings. Thought has great power. Those who serve in hospitals seldom fall ill, because of their confident attitude. They are vitalized by their energy and strong thoughts.

For this reason, as you get older, it is best not to tell others your age. As soon as you do, they see that age in you and associate it with diminishing health and vitality. The thought of advancing age creates anxiety, and thus you devitalize yourself. So keep your age private. Say to God: "I am immortal. I am blessed with the privilege of good health, and I thank Thee."

Therefore be cautious, but not fearful. Take the precaution of going on a purifying diet now and then, so that any conditions of illness that may be present in the body will be eliminated. Do your best to remove the causes of illness and then be absolutely unafraid. There are so many germs everywhere that if you began to fear them you would not be able to enjoy life at all. Even with all your sanitary precautions, if you could look at your home through a microscope you would lose all desire to eat!

Techniques of Tuning Out Fear

Whatever it is that you fear, take your mind away from it and leave it to God. Have faith in Him. Much suffering is due simply to worry. Why suffer now when the malady has not yet come? Since most of our ills come through fear, if you give up fear you will be free at once. The healing will be instant.

Every night, before you sleep, affirm: "The Heavenly Father is with me; I am protected." Mentally surround yourself with Spirit and His cosmic energy and think: "Any germ that attacks me will be electrocuted." Chant *"Aum"* three times,* or the word "God." This will

---

*In the scriptures of India, *Aum (Om)* is the basis of all sounds; the universal symbol-word for God. *Aum* of the Vedas became the

shield you. You will feel His wonderful protection. Be fearless. It is the only way to be healthy. If you commune with God His truth will flow to you. You will know that you are the imperishable soul.

Whenever you feel afraid, put your hand over your heart, next to the skin; rub from left to right, and say, "Father, I am free. Tune out this fear from my heart radio." Just as you tune out static on an ordinary radio, so if you continuously rub the heart from left to right, and continuously concentrate on the thought that

---

sacred word *Hum* of the Tibetans; *Amin* of the Moslems; and *Amen* of the Egyptians, Greeks, Romans, Jews, and Christians. *Amen* in Hebrew means *sure, faithful. Aum* is the all-pervading sound emanating from the Holy Ghost (Invisible Cosmic Vibration; God in His aspect of Creator); the "Word" of the Bible; the voice of creation, testifying to the Divine Presence in every atom. In the *Self-Realization Fellowship Lessons,* Paramahansa Yogananda teaches techniques of meditation whose practice brings direct experience of God as *Aum* or Holy Ghost. That blissful communion with the invisible divine Power ("the Comforter, which is the Holy Ghost"—John 14:26) is the truly scientific basis of prayer.

you want to tune out fear from your heart, it will go; and the joy of God will be perceived.

Fear Ceases With the Contact of God

Fear is constantly haunting you. Cessation of fear comes with the contact of God, nothing else. Why wait? Through yoga you can have that communion with Him....

When I started in this path, my life at first was chaotic; but as I kept on trying, things began to clear up for me in a marvelous way. Everything that happened showed me that God *is,* and that He can be known in this life. When you find God, what assurance and fearlessness you will have! Then nothing else matters at all, nothing can ever make you afraid. Thus did Krishna exhort Arjuna to face fearlessly the battle of life and become spiritually victorious: "Surrender not to unmanliness; it is unbecoming to thee. O Scorcher of Foes, forsake this small weakheartedness! Arise!"*

*Bhagavad Gita II:3.

THE FEARLESS MIND AND THE HEALTHY BODY

A retelling of a traditional fable

While meditating late one night, a certain saint saw the ghost of the dread smallpox disease entering the village where he lived. "Stop, Mr. Ghost!" he cried. "Go away. You must not molest a town in which I worship God."

"I will take only three people," the ghost replied, "in accordance with my cosmic karmic duty." At this the saint unhappily nodded assent.

The following day three persons died of smallpox. But the next day several more died, and each day thereafter more villagers were overcome by the fearful disease. Thinking that a great deception had been played on him, the saint meditated deeply and summoned the ghost. When it came, the saint rebuked it.

"Mr. Ghost, you deceived me and did not speak the truth when you said you would take only three people with your smallpox."

But the ghost replied, "By the Great Spirit, I did speak the truth to you."

The saint persisted. "You promised to take only three persons, and scores have succumbed to the disease."

"I took only three," said the ghost. "The rest killed themselves with fear."

You must resurrect your mind from the consciousness of disease—from the thought of disease. You are the invulnerable Spirit; but the body now rules the mind. The mind must rule the body....

What are you afraid of? You are an immortal being. You are neither a man nor a woman, as you may think, but a soul, joyous, eternal.

❧

May I Overcome Fear

(A Prayer)

Teach me to overcome fear by understanding its uselessness. May I not anesthetize with forebodings my unlimited ability as Thy child to meet successfully any test of life.

Free me from paralyzing dreads. May I not visualize accidents and calamities, lest by the power of thought I invite them to externalize themselves.

Inspire me to put my trust in Thee, not in human precautions only. I can pass safely where bullets fly or dread bacteria abound if I realize Thou art ever with me.

May I never tremble at the thought of death. Help me to remember that for this body the Summoner shall arrive only once; and that, through his mercy, when my time is come I shall not know of it nor care.

Teach me, O Infinite Spirit! that whether I am awake or asleep, alert or daydreaming, living or dying, Thine all-protecting presence encircles me.

—*from* Whispers from Eternity

RIDDING THE CONSCIOUSNESS OF WORRY

Worry is a psychophysical state of consciousness in which you are caught in feelings of helplessness and apprehension about some trouble you don't know how to get rid of. Perhaps you are seriously concerned about your child, or your health, or a mortgage payment. Not finding an immediate solution, you start worrying about the situation. And what do you get? A headache, nervousness, heart trouble. Because you do not clearly analyze yourself and your problems, you do not know how to control your feelings or the condition that con-

Extracts from a talk given at Self-Realization Fellowship Temple, Encinitas, California. The complete talk appears in *The Divine Romance* (Paramahansa Yogananda's *Collected Talks and Essays, Volume II*).

fronts you. Instead of wasting time worrying, think positively about how the cause of the problem can be removed. If you want to get rid of a trouble, calmly analyze your difficulty, setting down point by point the pros and cons of the matter; then determine what steps might be best to accomplish your goal.

Face Financial Difficulties With Fearlessness and Creativity

If you have no money, you feel forsaken; the whole world seems to be going backward. But worry will not provide a solution. Get busy and make this determination: "I will shake the world to get my share. In order to keep me quiet, the world must satisfy my need." Each person who has performed some work, even clearing away weeds, has done something worthwhile on earth. Why shouldn't everyone receive his just share of the earth's bounty? No one need starve or be left out.

The present money standard will go; remember what I say. Money creates a desire for power, and too often it makes the possessor heartless to the sufferings of others. Accumulation of wealth is all right if the wealthy person also has the desire to help others in their need. Money is a boon in the possession of unselfish people, but it is a curse in the hands of the selfish. I used to know a man in Philadelphia who was worth ten million dollars, but it never gave him happiness; it brought him only misery. And he wouldn't even buy a ten-cent cup of coffee for anyone else. Gold has been given for our use, but it belongs to no one save the Divine Spirit. Each child of God has a right to use God's gold. You must not admit failure and give up your right.

God made you His son. You have made yourself a beggar. If you have convinced yourself that you are a helpless mortal, and you allow everyone else to convince you that you can't get a job, then you have passed the decree in your own mind that you are down and done for. No judgment from God or fate, but your own pronouncement on yourself, keeps you poor or worried. Success or failure is determined in your own mind.

Even against the negative opinion of the rest of society, if you bring out by your all-conquering God-given will the conviction that you cannot be left to suffer in difficulties, you will feel a secret divine power coming upon you; and you will see that the magnetism of that conviction and power is opening up new ways for you.

Do not grieve over your present state, and do not worry. If you refuse to worry, and if you make the right effort, you will remain calm and you will surely find a way of reaching your goal.

Remember that every time you worry, you put on a mental brake; and in struggling against that resistance, you place strain on your heart and mind. You wouldn't try to drive off in your car with the brake on, because you know it would severely damage the mechanism. Worry is the brake on the wheels of your efforts; it brings you to a dead stop. Nothing is impossible, unless you think it is. Worry can convince you that it is impossible to do what you want to do.

Worrying wastes time and energy. Use your mind instead to try to make some positive effort. It is even better to be a go-getting materialistic man and accomplish something, than to be lazy; the lazy man is forsaken by both man and God. Many fortunes have been made by enterprising people, but don't make money your criterion of success. Often it isn't the money, but the creative ability exercised in earning it, that brings satisfaction.

A Clear Conscience:
Key to Fearless Living

It is foolish to try to flee from your worries, for wherever you go, your worries go with you. You must learn to face your problems fearlessly and with a clear conscience, as I have done.

35

Now I have no more prayers for my soul or my body, for I have achieved eternal assurance from God. This is sufficient. For me, to pray would be to doubt. My conscience is free, for I have done no wrong to any human being. I know this to be truth. To be able to say to oneself, "I have wronged no one," is to be the happiest person on earth. . . .

Be a friend to all. Even if your love and trust are betrayed by some, don't worry. Always be yourself; you are what you are. This is the only sincere way to live. Though all may not want to be your friend, you should befriend all, never expecting anything in return. I understand and love all, but I never expect of anyone that he should be my friend and understand me. On the strength of this principle, I am at peace with myself and the world, and never feel any cause for worry.

The treasure of friendship is your richest possession, because it goes with you beyond this life. All the true friends you have made you will meet again in the home of the Father, for real love is never lost. On the other hand, hate is never lost, either. Whatever you hate, you also attract to yourself again and again until you overcome that intense dislike....

You must not hate even your enemies. No one is all bad. If you hear someone playing a piano that has a defective key, you are inclined to judge the whole piano as bad. But the fault lies in just one key. Fix it, and you will see that the piano is perfectly good. God lives within all His children. To hate anyone is to deny Him in yourself and in others. This earth is the laboratory of God. We burn ourselves in the fire of mortal experience so that our divine immortality, which is buried beneath the dross of our consciousness, may be once again revealed. Love all, keep your own counsel, and do not worry.

Give your troubles to God. When you worry, it is your funeral, all arranged by yourself. You don't want to be buried alive by your anxieties! Why suffer and die every day from worry? No matter what you are going through —poverty, sorrow, ill health—remember that somebody on this earth is suffering a hundred times more than you are. Do not consider yourself so unfortunate, for thus you defeat yourself, and close out the omnipotent light of God that is ever seeking to help you....

Titiksha: The Art of Mental Endurance

No sensation or mental torture can affect you if the mind is dissociated from it and anchored in the peace and joy of God.

Evenminded endurance is called *titiksha* in Sanskrit. I have practiced this mental neutrality. I have sat and meditated all night long in icy water in bitterly cold weather. Similarly, I have sat from morning till evening on the burning hot sands in India. I gained great mental strength by doing so. When you have practiced such self-discipline, your mind becomes impervious to all disturbing circumstances. If you think you can't do something, your mind is a slave. Free yourself.

I don't mean that you should be rash. Try to rise above disturbances gradually. Endurance is what you must have. Whatever may be your trouble, make a supreme effort to remedy it without worry; and until it is resolved, practice *titiksha*. Isn't this practical wisdom? If you are young and strong, then as you gradually strengthen your will and mind you can practice more rigid methods of self-discipline as I did.

If you are thinking that the winter weather is coming, and you are bound to catch cold, you are not developing mental strength. You have already committed yourself to certain weakness. When you feel you are susceptible to catching a cold, mentally resist: "Get away! I am following commonsense precautions, but I will not allow worry about it to invite the illness by weakening my mind." This is the right mental attitude. In your heart, sincerely do your best at all times, but without anxiety. Worry only paralyzes your efforts. If you do your best, God will reach down His hand to help you....

Remember that the mind cannot suffer any pain unless it accepts the suggestion of pain. Mind cannot suffer from poverty or anything else unless it accepts the unpleasantness of the condition. Jesus was severely treated—his life was filled with problems, obstacles, and uncertainties—yet he had no worries. Remember, you also are a son of God. You may be forsaken by everyone else, but you cannot be forsaken by God, because He loves you. You should never worry, because God made you in His indomitable image....

Realize that the infinite presence of the Heavenly Father is ever within you. Tell Him: "In life and death, health and sickness, I worry not, O Lord, for I am Thy child evermore."

THE LION WHO
BECAME A SHEEP

A retelling of a traditional story from India

Once there was a huge lioness, pregnant and half-starved. As the days passed and the baby lion grew heavier within her, she had a hard time moving around in quest of prey. Even when the lioness successfully stalked some creature she wasn't quick enough to pounce, and so failed every time to capture her prey.

Roaring with sadness, heavy with the baby lion, and pining with hunger, the lioness roamed through the forest and finally fell asleep in the shade of a grove of trees bordering a pasture. As she was dozing, she dreamed that she saw a flock of sheep grazing. Trying to pounce upon one of the dream sheep, she jerked and woke up to behold in reality a large flock of sheep grazing nearby.

Overwhelmed with joy, forgetful of the baby lion she was carrying inside her, and impelled by the madness of unappeased hunger, the lioness pounced upon a young lamb and disappeared into the depths of the jungle. The lioness did not even realize that, owing to the severe exertion of her mad leap for the lamb, she had given birth to her cub.

The sheep were paralyzed with fear at the attack, but when the lioness departed and the panic was over, they wakened from their stupor and noticed the loss of the lamb. As the flock bleated out lamentations in sheep language they noticed, to their great astonishment, the helpless baby lion mewling in their midst. One of the ewes took pity on the cub and adopted it as her own.

Several years passed; the orphan lion, now a mature beast with long mane and tail, roamed with the flock behaving exactly like a sheep. Bleating instead of roaring, and eating grass instead of meat, this strictly vegetarian lion had perfected himself in the weakness and meekness of a lamb.

It so happened that one day another lion strolled out of the nearby forest which opened into the green pasture and to his delight beheld the flock of sheep. Thrilled with joy and whipped by hunger, the strong lion pursued the fleeing flock of sheep, when, to his great amazement, he noticed the husky sheep-lion, tail high in the air, also fleeing at top speed ahead of the sheep.

The pursuing lion paused for a moment, switching his tail in astonishment and pondering within himself: "I can understand sheep flying away from me, but I cannot imagine why a stalwart lion should run too. This runaway lion interests me." Spurred by determination to get to the fleeing lion, he raced hard and pounced upon the escaping beast. The sheep-lion fainted with fear. The other lion was more puzzled than ever. Slapping the sheep-lion out of his swoon, he rebuked him in a hoarse voice: "Wake up! What's the matter? Why do you, a brother lion, fly away from me?"

The sheep-lion closed his eyes and bleated out in sheep language: "Please let me go. Don't kill me! I am just a sheep from yonder flock that fled away and left me."

"Aha! Now I see why you are bleating," said his captor. He pondered a moment, then seized the mane of the sheep-lion with his mighty jaws, and dragged him toward a lake at the end of the pasture land. When they reached the shore of the lake, he pushed the deluded creature's head over the water so that it was reflected there, and began to shake him violently, for the sheep-lion still had his eyes tightly closed. "What's the matter with you?" asked his captor. "Open your eyes and see that you are not a sheep."

"Bleat, bleat, bleat! Please don't kill me. Let me go! I am not a lion, but only a poor meek sheep," wailed the silly beast. The other lion, angry now, gave his captive a terrible shake. Under the impact of it, the sheep-lion opened his eyes and was astonished to see in the water a reflection, not of a sheep's head, as he expected, but a lion's head, like that of the one who was shaking him with his paw. Then the big creature said in lion language: "Look at my face and your face reflected in the water. They are the same; and this voice of mine roars. It does not bleat. You must roar instead of bleating."

The sheep-lion, convinced, tried to roar, but at first succeeded only in producing bleat-mingled roars. But under the slapping paws and exhortation of his new friend, he at last succeeded in roaring effectively. Then both lions leaped across the fields....

The foregoing story fittingly illustrates how most of us, though made in the all-powerful

image of the Divine Lion of the Universe, remember only being born and brought up in the
sheepfold of mortal weakness. So we bleat with
fear at the predators of sickness, lack, sorrow,
and death, instead of roaring with immortality
and power and preying on mortal delusion and
ignorance.

Invincible Lion of the Self

A cub of the Divine Lion, somehow I found myself confined in a sheepfold of frailties and limitations. Fear-filled, living long with sheep, day after day I bleated. I forgot my affrighting bellow that banishes all enemy sorrows.

O Invincible Lion of the Self! Thou didst drag me to the water hole of meditation, saying: "Thou art a lion, not a sheep! Open thine eyes, and roar!"

After Thy hard shakings of spiritual urge, I gazed into the crystal pool of peace. Lo, I saw my face like unto Thine!

I know now that I am a lion of cosmic power. Bleating no more, I shake the error forest with reverberations of Thine almighty voice. In divine freedom I bound through the jungle of earthly delusions, devouring the little creatures of vexing worries and timidities, and the wild hyenas of disbelief.

O Lion of Liberation, ever send through me Thy roar of all-conquering courage!

—*from* Whispers from Eternity

THE WAY TO PERMANENT FEARLESSNESS:
EXPERIENCING YOUR IMMORTALITY THROUGH MEDITATION

Do you ever think that you have been completely unsettled by circumstances—ruffled, shattered, whipped, lacking power? Banish such thoughts! You have power; you do not use it. You have all the power you need. There is nothing greater than the power of the mind.

———◆———

How necessary it is to analyze why you behave the way you do. Some people are filled with fear; they have made it a chronic habit. They nurture fear every day; and therefore their days are miserable with worry and anxiety.

What is the logic of it? We are all going to die one day. It only happens once, and when it happens it is all over with. Then why be afraid of it? Why die every day through fear? When you learn to reason clearly, you discover that so many of your everyday attitudes and actions are foolish; the unhappiness they create is totally unnecessary.

———— • ————

It is true that man's ego is embodied only once under one personality and form. But although the ego successively relinquishes the individualities of its incarnations, it yet carries, within subconscious chambers, the pleasures and terrors of the experiences of all past lives. Each man feels within himself many subterranean fears that are rooted in dark experiences of lives long forgotten.

Those who spend their earthly sojourns in emotionally reacting to the endless dream pictures of life continue to behold turbulent dream pictures of death and new incarnations....By deep *samadhi* meditation, the haunting specters of man's inexplicable fears are eradicated.

———◆———

Resurrect your mind from the little habits that keep you worldly all the time. Smile that perpetual smile—that smile of God. Smile that strong smile of balanced recklessness—that million-dollar smile that no one can take from you....Live every second in the consciousness of your relationship with the Infinite.

———◆———

Realization that all power to think, speak, feel, and act comes from God, and that He is ever with us, inspiring and guiding us, brings an instant freedom from nervousness. Flashes of divine joy will come with this realization; some-times a deep illumination will pervade one's being, banishing the very concept of fear. Like an ocean, the power of God sweeps in, surging through the heart in a cleansing flood, removing all obstructions of delusive doubt, nervousness, and fear. The delusion of matter, the consciousness of being only a mortal body, is overcome by contacting the sweet serenity of Spirit, attainable by daily meditation. Then you know that the body is a little bubble of energy in His cosmic sea.

———•———

God made us angels of energy, encased in solids—with the current of life shining through the material bulb of flesh—but we are now concentrating upon the frailties and fragility of the bulb, and have forgotten how to feel the immortal, indestructible properties of the eternal life energy within the changeable flesh.

———•———

You are only dreaming that you have a body of flesh. Your real self is light and consciousness. You are not the physical body. The visibility of the body deludes our material consciousness. If you cultivate superconsciousness—awareness of your real self, the soul—you will realize that the body is simply a projection of that invisible self within. Then you can do anything with the body. But don't try just yet to walk on water!

———— •◆• ————

Religious effort must be applied to the conversion of our consciousness from its belief in a mortal, perishable body into realization that "solid" flesh is composed of immortal, imperishable energy "frozen" into a human form. And that form is sustained by God's intelligent Cosmic Energy within and around us. . . .

Pure energy cannot be hurt by automobile accidents, rheumatism, appendicitis, cancer, or tuberculosis—nor can it be stabbed by swords, shot by guns, or burnt by fire. We need practical religion to teach us how to become aware of ourselves as souls encased in bodies of luminous eternal energy.

———◆———

Turn the spotlight of your attention inward, away from the limited visible man. The physical body has backaches and stomachaches; it suffers deterioration in old age; it is the nastiest little animal! always crying and whining for something. The visible man cannot bear a bad fall, and he sometimes shrinks at even a pinprick; the invisible man is unhurt by anything. He is free. He can banish all the troubles of the physical body. The invisible man within you is what you are. "The One who pervades all things is imperishable. Nothing has power to destroy this Unchangeable Spirit."*

*Bhagavad Gita II:17.

You think you are the body, but you are not. A piece of ice can be melted into liquid and then made to disappear by evaporation. The process can be reversed, condensing the vapor into liquid and freezing the liquid into solid form as ice once again. The ordinary man has not yet learned to perform similar transformations with his bodily atoms, but Christ showed that it could be done....

We are coming to that evolutionary period during which we will realize increasingly that we are really invisible beings, or souls. To live only in the consciousness of this visible body of flesh is spiritually retarding, for the body is subject to the sufferings of disease, injury, poverty, hunger, and death. We should not desire to think of ourselves as this visible, vulnerable, destructible body. The invisible man within us cannot be hurt or killed. Should we not strive more to realize our unknown immortal nature? By increasing our knowledge of this invisible self we will be able to control the man visible, as great masters do. Even when the visible man is in distress, he who is aware of his divine powers as the invisible man within can remain detached from physical suffering.

How will you gain such control? First you must learn to live more in silence; you must learn to meditate. It may seem uninteresting at first; you have kept so closely in touch with this visible body that you have difficulty in thinking about anything except its ceaseless troubles, desires, and demands. But make the effort. Keeping your eyes closed, repeat again and again, "I am made in the image of God. My life cannot be destroyed by any means. I am the invisible man everlasting."

That invisible man is made in the image of God, free as the Spirit is free. In the visible man lie all the troubles and limitations of the world. Whenever we are conscious of our bodies we are tied to the body's limitations. Hence the great masters teach us to close our eyes and re-mind ourselves, by meditation on the invisible self, that we are not restricted to what our physical bodies can do....

In meditation you peer into the darkness behind closed eyes and center your attention on the soul, the invisible self within you. Learning to control your thoughts and interiorize your mind, by scientific guru-given techniques of meditation, you will gradually develop spiritually: your meditations will deepen and your invisible self, the soul-image of God within, will become real to you. In this joyous awakening of Self-realization, the limited body consciousness that was so real becomes unreal; and you know that you have found your true invincible self and its oneness with God.

———•———

Make a supreme effort to get to God. I am speaking practical truth to you, practical sense;

and giving you a philosophy that will take away all of your consciousness of hurt. Be afraid of nothing....

Meditate deeply and faithfully, and one day you will wake up in ecstasy with God and see how foolish it is that people think they are suffering. You and I and they are all pure Spirit.

———•◆•———

O Omnipresent Protector! when clouds of war send rains of gas and fire, be Thou my bomb shelter.

In life and death, in disease, famine, pestilence, or poverty may I ever cling to Thee. Help me to realize I am immortal Spirit, untouched by the changes of childhood, youth, age, and world upheavals.

—from Whispers from Eternity

FINDING INNER ASSURANCE
THAT GOD IS WITH YOU

The Sanskrit word for faith is wonderfully expressive. It is *visvas*. The common literal rendering, "to breathe easy; have trust; be free from fear," does not convey the full meaning. Sanskrit *svas* refers to the motions of breath, implying thereby life and feeling. *Vi* conveys the meaning of "opposite; without." That is, he whose breath, life, and feeling are calm, he can have faith born of intuition; it cannot be possessed by persons who are emotionally restless. The cultivation of intuitive calmness requires unfoldment of the inner life. When developed

---

Extracts from *Journey to Self-realization* (Paramahansa Yogananda's *Collected Talks and Essays, Volume III*).

sufficiently, intuition brings immediate comprehension of truth. You can have this marvelous realization. Meditation is the way.

Meditate with patience and persistence. In the gathering calmness, you will enter the realm of soul intuition. Throughout the ages, those beings who attained enlightenment were those who had recourse to this inner world of God-communion. Jesus said: "When thou prayest, enter into thy closet, and when thou hast shut thy door, pray to thy Father which is in secret; and thy Father which seeth in secret shall reward thee openly."* Go within the Self, closing the door of the senses and their involvement with the restless world, and God will reveal to you all His wonders.

———— ◆ ————

If you live with the consciousness that you are His child and that He is your Father, and

* Matthew 6:6.

make up your mind to do your best with dogged determination, then in spite of obstacles, and even if you make mistakes, His power will be there to help you out. I live by that law....

In San Francisco [in 1925], I had only $200 in the bank and was about to begin a lecture campaign. I had not enough money even to make a start; and many large bills had to be paid. I said: "God is with me. He has given me this trouble and He will look after me. I am doing His work; I know He will help me." If the whole world forsakes you, but you *know* that He is with you, His law will work its wonders for you.

When my secretary came to me and I told him how much we had in the bank, he literally collapsed on the floor. I said, "Get up." He was shaking: "We are going to jail for not paying our bills!" I said, "We are not going to jail. In seven days we will have all the money we need for the campaign."

He was a doubting Thomas, but I had faith.

I was not in need of money for any gain of my own, but to spread God's work. I had no fear, even for the enormity of my troubles. Fear is afraid of me. What is there to fear? Nothing should give you fear. Face all troubles with faith in God and you will conquer.

Bhagavad Gita says: "With heart absorbed in Me, and by My grace, thou shalt overcome all impediments."* And think of it! I was walking in front of the Palace Hotel when an elderly woman came up to me and said, "Can I talk with you?" We exchanged a few words and then out of the blue she said, "I have money to burn. Can I help you?"

I replied, "I don't need your money. Why should you offer money to me when you don't even know me?"

She answered, "But I do know you; I have heard so much about you." And right there she

*XVIII:58.

wrote out a check for $27,000. I saw in that the hand of God....

I live by faith in God. My power is God. I do not believe in any other power. As I concentrate on that Power, it works through me.... That power of God is working with you also. You will see it is so if you have faith and know that prosperity comes not from material sources but from God.

The Lord doesn't tell you that you do not have to think for yourself, nor that you need not use your initiative. You have to do your part. The point is, if you cut yourself off from the Source by wrong actions and desires, and by lack of faith and divine communion, then you cannot receive His all-powerful help. But if you are guided by attunement with God, He will help you to do the right thing, and to avoid mistakes.

The way to start is by deep and regular morning and evening meditation. The more you meditate, the more you will realize there is Something behind the kingdom of ordinary consciousness where a great peace and happiness reign. Practice the presence of this peace and happiness, for it is the first proof of God-contact. It is the conscious realization of Truth within yourself. That is what you need.

That is how to worship Truth; for we can worship only what we know. Most people worship God as Something intangible; but when you begin to worship Him as real, through your own inner perception, you will feel increasingly the presence of His power in your life. No matter what else you might do, nothing will produce that God-contact which comes from deep meditation. Fervent effort to increase the inner peace and happiness born of meditation is the only way to realize God.

The time to pray to God for guidance is after you have meditated and felt that inner peace and joy; that is when you have made divine contact. If you think you have a need, you can then place it before God and ask whether it is a legitimate prayer. If you feel inwardly that your need is just, then pray: "Lord, you know that this is my need. I will reason, I will be creative, I will do whatever is necessary. All I ask of You is that You guide my will and creative abilities to the right things that I should do."

Be fair with God. Perhaps He has something better for you than what you are praying for. It is a fact that sometimes your most fervent prayers and desires are your greatest enemies. Talk sincerely and justly with God, and let Him decide what is right for you. If you are receptive, He will lead you, He will work with you. Even if you make mistakes, don't be afraid. Have faith. Know that God is with you. Be guided in everything by that Power. It is unfailing. This truth is applicable to every one of you.

FEARLESSNESS MEANS FAITH IN GOD

Fearlessness is the impregnable rock on which the house of spiritual life must be erected. Fearlessness means faith in God: faith in His protection, His justice, His wisdom, His mercy, His love, His omnipresence....

Fear robs man of the indomitability of his soul. Disrupting Nature's harmonious workings emanating from the source of divine power within, fear causes physical, mental, and spiritual disturbances. Extreme fright can even stop the heart and bring sudden death. Long-continued anxieties give rise to psychological complexes and chronic nervousness.

Fear ties the mind and heart (feeling) to the external man, causing the consciousness to be identified with mental or physical nervousness, thus keeping the soul concentrated on the ego, the body, and the objects of fear. The devotee should discard all misgivings, realizing them to be stumbling blocks that hinder his concentration on the imperturbable peace of the soul....

Death is perhaps the ultimate challenge of faith in mortal man. Fear of this inevitability is foolish. It comes only once in a lifetime; and after it has come the experience is over, without having affected our true identity or diminished in any way our real being.

Illness, also, is a gauntlet tossed at the feet of faith. An ill person should try earnestly to rid himself of his malady. Then, even if doctors proclaim there is no hope, he should remain tranquil, for fear shuts the eyes of faith to the omnipotent, compassionate Divine Presence. Instead of indulging anxiety he should affirm: "I am ever safe in the fortress of Thy loving care." A fearless devotee, succumbing to an incurable disease, concentrates on the Lord and becomes ready for liberation from the bodily prison into a glorious afterlife in the astral world. Thereby he advances closer to the goal of supreme liberation in his next life. A man who dies in terror, having surrendered to despair his faith in God and the remembrance of his immortal nature, carries with him into his next incarnation that bleak pattern of fear and weakness; this imprint may well attract to him similar calamities—a continuation of a karmic lesson not yet learned. The heroic devotee, however, though he may lose the battle with death, yet wins the war of freedom. All men are meant to realize that soul consciousness can triumph over every external disaster.

When subconscious fears repeatedly invade the mind, in spite of one's strong mental resistance, it is an indication of some deep-seated karmic pattern. The devotee must strive even harder to divert his attention by infusion of his conscious mind with thoughts of courage. Further, and most important, he should confide himself completely into God's trustworthy hands. To be fit for Self-realization, man must be fearless.

———◆———

The Highest Faith:
Fearless Surrender to God

Life, its substance and purpose, is an enigma, difficult yet not unknowable. With our progressive thinking, we are daily solving some of its secrets....But in spite of all our devices and strategies and inventions, it seems we are still playthings in the hands of destiny, and have a long way to go before we can be independent of nature's domination.

To be constantly at the mercies of nature— surely that is not freedom. Our enthusiastic minds are rudely seized by a sense of helplessness when we are victimized by floods, tornadoes, or earthquakes; or when, apparently without rhyme or reason, illness or accident snatches our dear ones from our bosom. It is then that we know we really haven't conquered much. In spite of all our efforts to make life what we want it to be, there will always remain certain conditions introduced on this planet—infinite and guided by an unknown Intelligence, operating without our initiative—which preclude our control....With all our certainties, we still have to abide an uncertain existence....

Hence comes the necessity of a fearless reliance on our true immortal Self and on the Supreme Deity in whose image that Self is made—a faith that acts without egoism, and plods on merrily, knowing no trepidation or constraint.

Exercise absolute fearless surrender to that Higher Power. Never mind that today you make the resolution that you are free and undaunted, and then tomorrow you catch the flu and become miserably sick. Don't weaken! Command your consciousness to remain steadfast in its faith. The Self cannot be contaminated by sickness. Maladies of the body come to you through the law of self-created habits of ill health lodged in your subconscious mind. Such karmic manifestations do not disprove the efficacy, the dynamic power, of faith.

Hold to the helm of faith, and mind not the buffeting of untoward circumstances. Be more furious than the fury of misfortune, more audacious than your dangers. The more this newfound faith will work its dynamic influence on you, the more your slavery to weakness will wane proportionately.

Not a corpuscle of blood can move, nor a puff of breath enter your nostrils, without the commandment of the Lord. Hence, absolute surrender to God is the criterion of faith. This surrender is not laziness, expecting God to do everything for you—your utmost effort to

bring about the desired result is also necessary
—rather, it is a surrender through love for God
and veneration of His supremacy.

———•———

My work is fulfilled when I have awakened
in you even the tiniest spark of the love I feel for
my Father. [In my youth] it took a great deal of
time to get acquainted with Him; it seemed in
this life I would never be able to succeed, for the
mind was so restless. But as often as the mind
tried to trick me into abandoning my meditation, I would trick the mind: "I will sit here, no
matter what noises or distractions come. I care
not if I have to die trying; I will keep on to the
end." As I persevered in this way, once in a while
a glimpse of the Divine Spirit would come; like
a spark, so near and yet so far, appearing and
then flitting away. But I stayed resolute. How I
waited! with infinite determination in the invisible silence. The deeper the concentration be-

71

came, the clearer and stronger became His assurance. Now He is with me always.

Blessed you are that you are hearing the message divine, the message of Spirit, the message that solves the mystery of the universe. What fear have you? Cast out all fear! There is nothing to be afraid of anymore when you have touched the Great Power of Spirit, which controls the very forces of creation, all the machinery of this universe. What greater hope could you have, what greater security could you seek, than the contact of the Infinite Being that is the essence of all that exists?...

He is the only harbor of safety from the storms of this world. "Take shelter in Him with all the eagerness of thy heart. By His grace thou shalt obtain the utmost peace and the Eternal Shelter."* In Him I have found the joy of my life, the indescribable blessedness of my

---

* Bhagavad Gita XVIII:62.

existence, the wonderful realization of His everywhereness right within me. I want you all to have that.

EPILOGUE

"Stand Unshaken Amidst the Crash of Breaking Worlds"

As time marches on, you must eventually realize that you are a part of the great One. Make God-realization your goal. Mahavatar Babaji said that even a little bit of this *dharma* —righteous action, seeking to know God— will save you from dire fears.*

The prospect of death, or of failure or other grievous troubles, awakens in man a great dread. When you are helpless to help yourself, when your family cannot do anything for you, when no one else can give you aid, what then is

---

*Paraphrasing the Bhagavad Gita, II:40. Mahavatar Babaji, first in the lineage of God-illumined masters behind Paramahansa Yogananda, often quoted this verse in referring to *Kriya Yoga*.

the state of your mind? Why allow yourself to be put in such a position? Find God, and anchor yourself in Him.

Before anyone else was with you, who was with you? God. And when you leave this earth, who will be with you? Only God. But you won't be able to know Him then unless you make friends with Him now. If you deeply seek God, you will find Him.

———— ◆ ————

The time has come for you to know and understand the purpose of religion: how to contact that supernal Joy, which is God, the great and eternal Comforter. If you can find that Joy, and if you can retain that Joy all the time, no matter what happens in your life, you will stand unshaken amidst the crash of breaking worlds.

———— ◆ ————

Do not be afraid of anything. Even when

tossing on a wave in a storm, you are still on the bosom of the ocean. Always hold on to the consciousness of God's underlying presence. Be of even mind, and say: "I am fearless; I am made of the substance of God. I am a spark of the Fire of Spirit. I am an atom of the Cosmic Flame. I am a cell of the vast universal body of the Father. 'I and my Father are One.'"

About the Author

Paramahansa Yogananda (1893–1952) is widely regarded as one of the preeminent spiritual figures of our time. Born in northern India, he came to the United States in 1920, where for more than thirty years he taught India's ancient science of meditation and the art of balanced spiritual living. Through his acclaimed life story, *Autobiography of a Yogi,* and his numerous other books, Paramahansa Yogananda has introduced millions of readers to the perennial wisdom of the East. Under the guidance of one of his earliest and closest disciples, Sri Daya Mata, his spiritual and humanitarian work is carried on by Self-Realization Fellowship, the international society he founded in 1920 to disseminate his teachings worldwide.

Also published by Self-Realization Fellowship...

Autobiography of a Yogi
by Paramahansa Yogananda

This acclaimed autobiography is at once a riveting account of an extraordinary life and a penetrating and unforgettable look at the ultimate mysteries of human existence. Hailed as a landmark work of spiritual literature when it first appeared in print, it remains one of the most widely read and respected books ever published on the wisdom of the East.

With engaging candor, eloquence, and wit, Paramahansa Yogananda narrates the inspiring chronicle of his life—the experiences of his remarkable childhood, encounters with many saints and sages during his youthful search throughout India for an illumined teacher, ten years of training in the hermitage of a revered yoga master, and the thirty years that he lived and taught in America. He records as well his meetings with Mahatma Gandhi, Rabindranath Tagore, Luther Burbank, the Catholic stigmatist Therese Neumann, and other celebrated spiritual personalities of East and West. Also included is extensive material that he added after the first edition came out in 1946, with a final chapter on the closing years of his life.

Considered a modern spiritual classic, *Autobiography of a Yogi* offers a profound introduction to the ancient science of yoga. It has been translated into many languages and is widely used in college and university courses. A perennial best-seller, the book has found its way into the hearts of millions of readers around the world.

————•◆•————

"A rare account." — The New York Times

"A fascinating and clearly annotated study."
—Newsweek

"There has been nothing before, written in English or in any other European language, like this presentation of Yoga."
—Columbia University Press

Other Books by Paramahansa Yogananda

Available at bookstores or directly from the
publisher (www.yogananda-srf.org)

Autobiography of a Yogi *(Audiobook, read by Ben Kingsley)*

God Talks With Arjuna: The Bhagavad Gita
(A New Translation and Commentary)

The Second Coming of Christ: The Resurrection of
the Christ Within You (A revelatory commentary
on the original teachings of Jesus)

The Collected Talks and Essays
Volume I: Man's Eternal Quest
Volume II: The Divine Romance
Volume III: Journey to Self-realization

Wine of the Mystic: The Rubaiyat of Omar Khayyam
—A Spiritual Interpretation

The Science of Religion

Whispers from Eternity

Songs of the Soul

Sayings of Paramahansa Yogananda

Scientific Healing Affirmations

Where There Is Light: Insight and Inspiration for
Meeting Life's Challenges

In the Sanctuary of the Soul:
A Guide to Effective Prayer

Inner Peace: How to Be Calmly Active and Actively Calm

How You Can Talk With God

Metaphysical Meditations

The Law of Success

To Be Victorious in Life

Why God Permits Evil and How to Rise Above It

Cosmic Chants

Self-Realization Fellowship Lessons

The scientific techniques of meditation taught by Paramahansa Yogananda, including *Kriya Yoga*—as well as his guidance on all aspects of balanced spiritual living—are presented in the *Self-Realization Fellowship Lessons*. For further information, you are welcome to write for the free booklet *Undreamed-of Possibilities*.

SELF-REALIZATION FELLOWSHIP
3880 San Rafael Avenue • Los Angeles, CA 90065-3298
TEL *(323) 225-2471* • FAX *(323) 225-5088*
www.yogananda-srf.org